EDITOR: MARTIN WINDROW

 OSPREY MILITARY · MEN-AT-ARMS SERIES

THE MONGOLS

W9-AIJ-598

Text by
S R TURNBULL

Colour plates by
RIDE

First published in Great Britain in 1980 by
Osprey, an imprint of Reed Consumer Books Ltd.
Michelin House, 81 Fulham Road,
London SW3 6RB
and Auckland, Melbourne, Singapore and Toronto

ISBN 0 85045 372 0

Filmset in Great Britain
Printed through World Print Ltd, Hong Kong

This book is dedicated to my son Alexander, who
likes reading about soldiers.

The author would like to extend his thanks to his
colleagues in the North Cheshire Military Modelling
Society for help and suggestions in connection with
this book.

The Rise of the Mongols

The history of the Mongol armies is a catalogue of superlatives. No armies in history have ever won so many battles or conquered so much territory. No army has ever provoked such justifiable terror and loathing in its victims, or slaughtered so many of its vanquished. No other army has made and later carried out to the letter strategic plans so grand as those conceived at the great *kuriltai* or Council of War in 1235, with simultaneous attacks on both Poland and Korea. What other army in history has marched on Russia in the winter and survived, let alone won victories? What other army, indeed, could have attacked Russia in winter by choice, because the frozen rivers and deep snow made communications easier?

These are the achievements that have made the Mongols the object of admiration and loathing ever since they erupted on to the world scene in 1206 when Genghis Khan, 'under the command and guidance of heaven', set out to conquer the world. It was a world far wider than that subdued by the great Alexander, who, we are told, wept because he had no world left to conquer. By the end of the 13th century Mongol armies had been in action in countries as far apart as Poland, Japan, Hungary, Russia, Palestine, Persia, India, Burma and Vietnam. Teutonic knights of Germany, and samurai of Japan, while ignorant of each other's existence, had in fact fought a common enemy.

The story of the Mongol armies begins with Genghis Khan, who was born in *c.*1167 in the wild steppe-land of Mongolia, where it is winter for nine months of the year and the fierce winds almost blow a rider off his horse. The child who was to become the Great Khan was the son of a warrior called Yesugei, who had captured an enemy called Temujin, and in the custom of the time bestowed this name upon his new-born son. When Temujin was nine years old Yesugei was poisoned by rivals, and, as the Mongols would not submit to the rule of a boy, Temujin, with his mother and family, was exiled from the tribe. The boy was now a fugitive, and led many exciting adventures which demonstrated his future military promise. In the fullness of time he came back in strength to claim his inheritance, making political alliances and defeating rivals. In 1204 he summoned a *kuriltai* to plan the campaign which was to give him supreme power over all the nomad tribes, and in 1206 he received the title 'Genghis Khan', acknowledging him as the ruler over 'all who dwell in felt tents'. It is from this date that the Mongol conquests begin.

If the Mongols had felt a certain affinity with their nomad neighbours in a common life-style which no doubt helped cement alliances, their relations with the nations of the south were historically those of confrontation, symbolized and realized by the Great Wall of China. China was at this time divided into three parts: the Sung in the south; the Ch'in in the north, whose capital was at Peking; and the smallest and weakest of the three, the Hsi-Hsia, on the western flank of the Great Wall. The Hsi-Hsia became the first civilized sedentary society to feel the force and fury of the Mongols, who crossed the Gobi Desert to attack them with huge success in 1211.

In the same year Genghis Khan was acquainted with the news that a new Ch'in emperor had ascended the throne, and that as a vassal Genghis Khan would be expected to make some public display of servitude. The Great Khan's reply was to turn to the south, spit on the ground, and order a general advance against the Ch'in Empire.

The war thus begun was to continue for 23 years, ending, after Genghis Khan's death, in the total destruction of the Ch'in. At first the campaign appeared to be no more than a series of raids through the Great Wall—but raids with a purpose beyond that of merely collecting booty. Soon Peking was threatened, and the Ch'in

Genghis Khan (1167–1227), from a Chinese portrait.

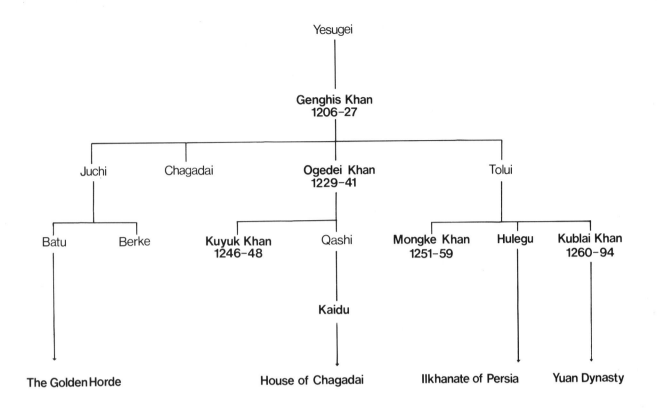

```
                              Yesugei
                                 │
                          Genghis Khan
                            1206-27
          ┌──────────┬────────────┼──────────────────┐
        Juchi      Chagadai    Ogedei Khan          Tolui
          │                      1229-41
      ┌───┴───┐              ┌──────┴──────┐     ┌──────┬──────────┐
    Batu    Berke        Kuyuk Khan     Qashi  Mongke Khan  Hulegu  Kublai Khan
                          1246-48               1251-59              1260-94
                                         │
                                       Kaidu
                                         │
  The Golden Horse          House of Chagadai   Ilkhanate of Persia   Yuan Dynasty
```

Family tree of the Mongol khans from Genghis to Kublai, including important princes mentioned in the text, and succeeding khanates.

emperor moved south. This desertion discouraged the defenders, and, with the help of skilled engineers pressed into Mongol service, Peking fell in 1215.

The conquest of China was interrupted at this point by the need to defeat an old enemy, a certain Kuchlug, who had fled from defeat at the hands of the Mongols during Genghis Khan's war of unification, and now lorded it over the Kara-Khitay Empire to the west. Genghis Khan entrusted the expedition to his general and old comrade Jebe, who performed his task with consummate loyalty and skill. One feature that was always to characterize Mongol warfare was the readiness with which responsibility was given to a general and the honourable manner in which it was accepted.

The defeat of the Kara-Khitay gave Genghis Khan a common frontier with the Shah of Khwarizm, a Muslim state stretching from modern Iran to the southern part of the Soviet Union in the neighbourhood of the Caspian and Aral seas. The Shah had executed a Mongol trade mission in 1218, believing, probably correctly, that they were spies. This was sufficient pretext for war, if pretext were needed; and in 1219 the Mongol hordes gathered to begin their first operation against a Muslim state. With excellent strategic foresight and execution Genghis Khan completely outflanked his enemies. Bokhara fell in 1220, to be followed shortly by Samarkand and Nishapur, every victory being accompanied by hideous slaughter on an immense scale. The Shah fled, pursued by the Mongol generals Jebe and Subadai, who harried him to his death.

An example of the confidence Genghis Khan had in his generals is shown by the campaign that followed. Having ensured the death of the Shah, Jebe and Subadai received permission for an armed reconnaissance in force, taking four *tumens* with them (one *tumen* was 10,000 men) on an extraordinary campaign through southern Russia. They wintered in Armenia and in the spring crossed the Caucasus Mountains, where they defeated a large army of Georgians who had gathered for the Fifth Crusade. They then crossed the Don and raided into the Crimea and

5

the Ukraine; but in 1223 their luck appeared to turn when they were attacked by 80,000 men under the Prince of Kiev and his Kipchak allies. After a feigned retreat the Mongols easily defeated them at the battle of the River Khalka, then returned to rendezvous with the main Mongol army after three years and 4,000 miles.

Meanwhile Genghis Khan had crossed the River Amou Daria and captured Balkh. In 1221 Merv was captured, and 700,000 people were murdered. In a manner that was to become commonplace in this war, the bloodiest of all that Genghis Khan conducted, none but useful artisans, especially siege engineers, was spared. At Merv the Mongol rearguard returned later to 'mop-up' any unfortunate civilians who had managed to escape the slaughter. The city was then destroyed so utterly that the site could have been ploughed upon, and in an extreme of vengeance for the death in battle of one of Genghis Khan's sons-in-law not even cats and dogs were left alive. In Herat 'no head was left on a body, nor body with a head'. Such atrocities led the Persian historian Juvaini to write: 'Even though there be generation and increase until the Resurrection the population will not attain to a tenth part of what it was before.'

In November 1221 the Persian campaign ended with a battle on the banks of the River Indus, where the defeated young prince, Jalal-al-din, son of the late Shah, cast off his armour and swam his horse across the river, a feat which impressed Genghis Khan.

From 1223 until 1225 the Khan spent a restful period hunting animals instead of people; but in 1226 his energies were once more turned against the Hsi-Hsia and the Ch'in, whose remnants had united against the Mongol yoke. While conducting the siege of a town called Ning-hsia Genghis Khan felt his death approaching and named his son Ogedei as his successor. The Great Khan died in 1227, and when Ning-hsia fell the entire population was slaughtered, in accordance with his dying wishes.

Unlike Genghis Khan's predecessor Attila the Hun, his great Empire did not die with him. After the defeat of the Ch'in a great *kuriltai* was held at which details were discussed for the

Mongols in long robes crossing a river. An illustration from Raschid-al-Din's *World History*. (Courtesy of Edinburgh University Library)

conquest of the Sung, the reduction of Korea, and the invasion of Europe.

The Mongol invasion of Europe, which occupied the great general Subadai from 1237 until 1242, is discussed in detail in the final chapter of this book as an example of a classic Mongol campaign.

As the years went by the successive Mongol khans became more convinced than ever that their supremacy had been ordained by heaven, and that at the name of the khan every knee should bow. The third khan, Kuyuk, reigned from 1246 until 1248, and his successor Mongke (1251–59) continued the Mongol conquests. In spite of the massacres carried out during the campaign against the Khwarizm Empire, Mongol power in Persian lands was limited to a few areas. The Abbasid caliphs held Baghdad, and a sect of Muslim heretics called the Ismai'ilis terrorized their neighbours from their fortresses in the Elburz Mountains. This group were also called the Assassins, from their use of the drug hashish, a term which has entered our own language as a synonym for cunning political murder.

To the peoples of Islam an attack on the Assassins by a Mongol army would have been seen as a glorious crusade, and it was hailed as

A nomad camp: an old Mongol illustration of a camp scene, showing equipment used by the Mongols.

such when it began in 1253. Once again we see the usual Mongol thoroughness of preparation. Two men out of every 10 in the Mongol forces were assigned to the army of campaign. A thousand engineers from China were brought to serve the catapults; pasture land was earmarked for future grazing; roads were repaired, and bridges built over rivers that would have to be crossed on the way. In the autumn of 1255 the army gathered near Samarkand in the most fearsome display of Mongol power seen since the days of Genghis Khan. As the advance began the Assassins cowered behind the walls of their castles perched like eagles' nests on the rocky peaks of mountains, and the Mongols began slowly and methodically to wipe out every member of the fanatical sect who had terrorized orthodox Muslims for two centuries.

Such was the rejoicing at the Assassins' downfall (Juvaini, the Persian historian, concludes his account of the campaign with the words, '. . . may God do likewise to all tyrants') that the inhabitants of Baghdad never once considered that they might be the next target for the barbarian onslaught. But the existence of a ruler such as

7

their caliph, who claimed authority over countless thousands, was such an insult to the Mongol world-view that he could not be allowed to continue the rivalry. In 1257 a message was sent to the young caliph, who composed a suitably arrogant reply, and within months Baghdad was surrounded. A week's bombardment by heavy catapults smashed one of the gate towers, and the Mongols flooded in to kill and loot for a further seven days. The story is told of how the caliph was shut up in a tower with all his gold and silver and left to starve to death in the midst of all his wealth. The legend is probably apocryphal; but it is true that the Mongol commanders, their professionalism offended, chided the caliph for not having spent some of his vast wealth on increasing the defences of the city.

This second Persian campaign shows how cunning the Mongols were at playing off one political faction or religious sect against another. The Muslims of Baghdad had hailed the Mongols as the destroyers of the Assassin heretics; now the Eastern Christians were to welcome the Mongols as the destroyers of a major centre of Islam. (Baghdad was in fact the richest city the Mongols

had ever captured.) One by one these Christian kingdoms began to explore the possibilities of an alliance with the Mongols against the Muslim infidels. The next stage of the Mongol advance, against Syria, was seen by the pious King of Armenia as a crusade. The strange warriors from the steppes may not have been Christians, but the fact that they were anti-Muslim was good enough reason for the king to place his entire army at their disposal.

This unholy alliance took the field in 1259. Aleppo fell to a violent catapult bombardment and suffered a six-day massacre. Damascus was abandoned, the Sultan Nasir fled to Egypt, and the Mongols entered without having to strike a blow. Their Christian allies joined them in a triumphal entry, forcing the defeated Muslims to carry the cross before them, and later turned one of the city's mosques into a Christian church.

The Mongols now turned their eyes towards the Mamluk sultans of Egypt. The wording and tone of the message they sent followed the familiar formula of 'bow down to the Khan or be destroyed', but by the time the message was delivered a dramatic development changed the situation. In 1259 Mongke Khan died; and just as the death of Ogedei had saved Europe in 1241 so this latest death saved Egypt. This time an armed conflict had broken out over the succes-

A Mongol pack-camel being led by a horseman. Note (centre) the characteristic hairstyle as described by European observers.

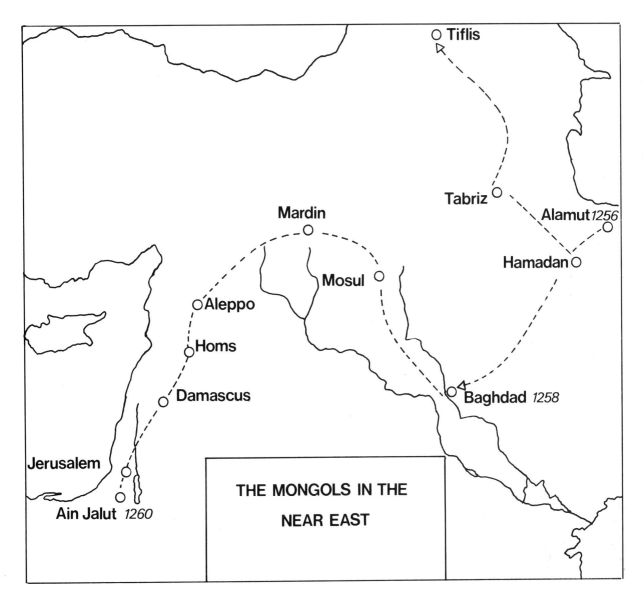

THE MONGOLS IN THE
NEAR EAST

The Mongol campaign in the Near East, showing the site of the battle of Ain Jalut.

sion, so Hulegu, the commander in the Near East, began to withdraw to the Mongol homelands.

Hearing of the Mongol retreat the Mamluk sultan sent an army to the north to follow the now-depleted Mongol forces. The armies met near Nazareth on 3 September 1260. The actual battle was fought at a spot called Ain Jalut, or Goliath's Spring, which was traditionally the site of David's defeat of the Philistine. Now the Mamluk David defeated the admittedly much-weakened Mongol Goliath. The political results of this unexpected reverse were far-reaching. A Mongol army had actually been defeated in battle. It was as if a spell had been broken.

In more ways than one the days of Mongol unity seemed to be over. Kublai became the fifth khan, but his influence never extended much further than China, and the Khanates that developed in Persia and Russia went very much their own ways.

Kublai Khan's triumph was the union of all China under his rule. The long struggle against the Sung, which Genghis Khan had begun, finished in 1276, and placed at the Khan's disposal the richest part of China. During this long campaign the influence of Chinese civilization had begun to affect the conquerors. Ogedei Khan had once boasted of his nation's military

9

Hulegu, the brother of Kublai Khan, and the commander in the Near Eastern campaign. (Reproduced by courtesy of the Trustees of the British Museum)

power, and received a perceptive reply from Ch'u-ts'ai, his Chinese adviser who had previously served under Genghis. 'The Empire was won on horseback,' said Ch'u-ts'ai, 'but it won't be governed on horseback.' The most striking evidence of the taming of the Mongols was the fact that the collapse of the Sung did not result in the utter destruction of China, but rather in the establishment of a Mongol ruling dynasty, the Yuan, and a break with the nomad tradition when the Mongol capital was moved from Karakorum to Peking.

One new resource that the Mongols now possessed was a large seagoing fleet, which meant that they could attempt to bring under submission the distant island kingdoms. The first country to feel the effects of a sea-borne Mongol army was Japan, in a campaign that was destined to prove the biggest disaster that any Mongol army suffered. Two invasions were attempted (which are recounted in detail in *The Samurai* by the present author), but neither succeeded in establishing more than a temporary bridgehead on the Japanese mainland.

The invasion of 1274 is interesting from the military point of view in that both sides in the conflict were fighting under unfamiliar circumstances. The Japanese, who had experienced no major wars for nearly a century, cherished an ideal of individual combat against worthy opponents, a mode of warfare entirely inappropriate when dealing with foreign invasion. The Mongols, whose army was composed largely of Chinese and Korean auxiliaries, had to fight on foot and thus abandon their well-tried mobile tactics, such as the feigned retreat.

In 1281 the Mongols returned with a much larger army, and once more skirmishes took place at the landing areas and on the boats themselves. But this time fate took a hand in the form of a fierce typhoon, which the Japanese immediately regarded as a heaven-sent ally. The storm completely wrecked the Mongol fleet, but as it was largely composed of Koreans on Korean ships its loss probably did not cause Kublai Khan much disturbed sleep.

The Mongols did not fare much better in South East Asia. This part of the world was at that time divided into four kingdoms: Annam and Champa, roughly corresponding to present-day

Vietnam; the Khmer Empire of Cambodia; and the Burmese Empire. In 1280 the ruler of Champa submitted to the Mongols following threats, but his people refused to allow their country to be divided up into Chinese administrative districts. A sea-borne invasion was launched in 1283, and the Vietnamese took to the hills and jungles to conduct a vigorous guerrilla campaign which lasted several years, and harassed several successive Mongol attempts at conquest.

In 1277 the Mongols turned their attentions towards Burma. Marco Polo has given us a lively account of the battle of Vochan in 1277, when the Mongols were confronted by Burmese war elephants, which he claims carried between 12 and 16 soldiers each. Whatever the number of troops they carried, the sight of the elephants alarmed the Mongol horses, so that the riders found them difficult to control. Fortunately the Mongol commander, who is not named, had the sense to order his men to dismount and tie their horses to the trees of a nearby forest. Taking their bows, which, as Marco Polo so rightly says, 'they know how to handle better than any troops in the world', they faced the elephants on foot, concentrating their deadly fire on the beasts themselves. Marco Polo continues:

'. . . When the elephants felt the smart of those arrows that pelted them like rain they turned tail and fled, and nothing on earth would have induced them to turn and face the Tartars. So off they sped with such a noise and uproar that you would have trowed the world was coming to an end! And then too they plunged into the wood and rushed this way and that, dashing their castles against the trees, bursting their harness and smashing and destroying everything that was on them.'

Seeing their enemies' confusion, the Mongols mounted their horses and charged in traditional Mongol style, and soon the Burmese were completely routed. But in spite of such victories on the battlefield it was not until 1297 that the Burmese finally acknowledged Mongol supremacy. Mongol influence continued to make itself felt as

An artist's impression of the fleet of Kublai Khan. After the defeat of the Sung the Mongols were able to launch sea-borne expeditions.

far south as Cambodia, which submitted meekly in 1296, and from 1294 the then two kingdoms of Siam became vassal states. Lastly, in 1293 Kublai sent an expeditionary force to Java. The Mongols captured the capital, but native resistance later forced them to withdraw. In Sumatra a petty prince recognized Mongol rule for a short while.

Such colonial expeditions were less important to Kublai Khan than the battles he was called upon to fight against rivals for the khanate. Opposition tended to come from those who had remained faithful to the old warrior traditions of the race, and had not been 'corrupted' by Chinese influence. Such a one was Kaidu, the grandson of Ogedei Khan, who proclaimed himself a legitimate heir and hoped at the very least to carve out some territory for himself in Mongolia. Wars with Kaidu continued intermittently from 1267 onwards. In 1287 Kaidu allied himself with Nayan, a Mongol prince of uncertain lineage who was a Nestorian Christian and carried the cross on his standards. Fortu-

nately for Kublai the two armies were widely separated, so he acted quickly before they had a chance of combining against him. Sending one army against Kaidu in the Karakorum area, Kublai set off to Manchuria to halt Nayan, and took advantage of his newly found naval strength to send the Imperial fleet from Chinese ports on the lower Yangtze to land huge quantities of supplies for the Khan's army at the mouth of the River Liao. Kublai was now 72 years old and suffered from rheumatism, but he kept considerable state in the field; he followed the battle, as befitted a Chinese emperor, from a wooden tower carried on four elephants. Marco Polo described it as:

'. . . a bartizan borne by four elephants, full of cross-bowmen and archers, with his flag high above him, bearing the figures of the sun and the moon, and so high that it could be seen from all sides. The four elephants were all covered with very stout boiled hides, overlaid with cloths of silk and gold.'

At first the battle seemed to go against Kublai's Sinicized Mongols. The Khan then drove his 'tower' on to a hill and ordered the *naccara* drums

Japanese samurai attack a Mongol ship during the attempted invasion of Japan.

Two Mongol warriors, fully armoured, grappling from the saddle. (Courtesy of the Bildarchiv Preussischer Kulturbesitz)

to be beaten, at which Nayan's army, which had been protected by a line of wagons, gave way before the attack. Marco Polo comments that the battle of the River Liao was one of the hardest the 'Tartars' ever fought.

It was also one of the last; the death of Kublai Khan in 1294, followed 10 years later by that of the Khan of Persia, marked the end of the era of Mongol imperialism. While Kublai had failed to conquer Japan his Persian kinsman had similarly failed to conquer Syria, and the march of Mongol conquest was never resumed. A wave of extraordinary energy had swept over the world in a hundred years, and had then settled down to leave its standard-bearers to be absorbed into the sedentary life-style of their new neighbours.

The Mongol Warrior

When considering the equipment, and in particular the personal appearance of the Mongols during the 13th century it is important to bear in mind that during these 100 years the Mongols evolved from rough and savage warriors to the army of a civilized state. Marco Polo in fact comments that the Sinicized Mongols were 'not what they had been'.

There is no shortage of information regarding the appearance of the typical Mongol warrior. Many European travellers noted the physical features, dress and weapons of the horsemen of the steppes, but some of these accounts have to be examined with care, as they range from careful eye-witness descriptions to pictures exaggerated by obvious fear and disgust. An example of the latter comes from the Persian poet Amir Khuzru, who describes several hundred Mongol prisoners taken by the Muslims:

'Their eyes were so narrow and piercing that they might have bored a hole in a brazen vessel, and their stench was more horrible than their colour. Their heads were set on their bodies as if they had no necks, and their cheeks resembled leather bottles full of wrinkles and knots. Their noses extended from cheekbone to cheekbone. Their nostrils resembled rotting graves, and from them the hair descended as far as the lips. Their moustaches were of extravagant length, but the beards about their chins were very scanty. Their chests, in colour half-black, half-white, were covered with lice which looked like sesame growing on a bad soil. Their bodies, indeed, were

A Mongol kills a rival. The Mongol skill at archery was renowned. (Courtesy of the Bildarchiv Preussischer Kulturbesitz)

covered with these insects, and their skins were as rough-grained as shagreen leather, fit only to be converted into shoes.'

John of Piano Carpini, who travelled as the Pope's ambassador to the Mongols between 1245 and 1247, has left us a more sober description of the people: '. . . In appearance the Tartars are quite different from all other men, for they are broader than other people between the eyes and across the cheekbones. Their cheeks also are rather prominent above their jaws; they have a flat and small nose, their eyes are little and their eyelids raised up to the eyebrows. For the most part, but with a few exceptions, they are slender about the waist; almost all are of medium height. Hardly any of them grow beards, although some have a little hair on the upper lip and chin and this they do not trim . . . They also have small feet.'

Their appearance was made more outlandish to Western eyes by some striking styles of hair-dressing. Friar William of Rubruck described how the Mongols shaved a square on top of their heads. This is confirmed by Carpini, who compared it to a monk's tonsure. From the front corners of this square, said William, they shaved seams down to their temples, which were also shaved as was the neck up to the point where it joins the skull, thus leaving a broken ring of hair round the head. The lock of hair left on the forehead was allowed to grow, and hung down as far as the eyebrows. The hair remaining on the scalp was wound into two plaits, which were knotted behind each ear. Carpini's description is similar. He also notes that they let the hair in the middle of the forehead grow longer than at the sides. Vincent de Beauvais' description of the shaving being in the shape of a horseshoe tallies well with the above accounts. All these descriptions refer to the period of about 1245.

The basic costume of the Mongols changed very little during the period under discussion. In general the garments worn were very practical, especially in the choice of furs and padded clothing for winter wear, which shows a firm grasp of the principles of insulation. The usual headgear was the Mongol cap, reproduced in many illustrations by contemporary artists. It was conical in shape, and made of quilted material or cloth, with a large turned-up brim which could be folded down in cold weather. Some styles had a brim divided in two. It was often decorated or lined with fox, wolf or lynx skin, or with plush. Some illustrations show a button or some projection at the point of the crown, and descriptions also speak of fur caps and earflaps. These earflaps may be just the brim, or they could indicate a different style. One later observer speaks of two red ribbons, each about 45cm long, hanging down at the back, but these are not mentioned by contemporary visitors. However, it seems reasonable to accept (for the 13th century) the same person's observations of a headcloth bound round the head and tied at the back, which was worn in the heat of summer.

The clothes worn were of a largely uniform pattern, consisting of a long robe-like coat which opened from top to bottom. The left breast doubled over the right, where it was fastened by a button or tie a few inches below the right armpit. It was also fastened on the left side, though this of course would not be seen. Some illustrations show the wide sleeves of this coat extending only to the elbow, exposing beneath it a shirt-like undergarment with long sleeves. These coats could be made of cotton for summer wear, but as the Mongol Empire increased, particularly into China and Persia, silk and metallic thread materials became available. The use of such fine cloths does not, however, automatically imply an elegant or luxurious appearance, which is unfortunately indicated by stylized Persian manuscripts. All travellers stress the Mongols' dirtiness, and many describe their habit of wiping their hands on their trousers or other clothes after they had eaten. The offensive smell of the Mongols has

Dismounted Mongol warriors (probably Chinese or Korean auxiliaries) firing on the retreat from a Japanese counter-attack. From the *Mongol Invasion Scroll*.

A model of a suit of Tibetan lamellar armour, which is strikingly similar to descriptions of Mongol armour. (The Armouries, H.M. Tower of London)

already been mentioned.

Their wide trousers were tucked into stout leather boots without heels and with thick soles made of felt. They were fastened by long laces.

In winter the robe would be augmented by thick felt socks and one or two fur coats. William of Rubruck states that they wore one with the fur in contact with them and the other with the fur outside, exposed to wind and snow. Furs were obtained from their subject peoples to the north and west, and well-to-do Mongols would wear outer garments made from the skins of wolves, foxes, or monkeys. The poor made do with dog or goat. They also wore trousers made of fur or skins, and the rich insulated their clothes with silk stuffing, which was very light, soft and warm. The poor lined their clothes with cotton cloth or with the fine wool they picked out of the coarser wool used for making felt. After the conquest of China silk underwear began to be worn.

Such clothing helped the Mongols to wage war in the depths of winter; but more important than clothing was the amazing hardiness of the warriors themselves. Marco Polo tells us that when the need arose they would go for 10 days without cooking food. On such occasions they could, if necessary, sustain themselves by drinking the blood of their horses, obtained by opening a vein in the animal's neck and letting the blood spurt into their mouths. Normal 'iron rations' for such campaigns would be 10lb of dried milk curd, two litres of *kumis* (an alcoholic drink made from fermented mare's milk), and some millet meal, or cured meat, which was tenderized by putting it under the horse's saddle and riding on it. In the morning half a pound of the dried milk curd would be mixed with water in one of the two leather bottles carried by the rider, and the shaking as he rode along would churn the mixture into the form of a watery yogurt.

The Mongol's liking for the milk of his horse added greatly to the range of his mobility. His appetite was equally far-ranging, and the usually reliable Carpini noted that they would eat dogs, wolves, foxes, horses, rats, mice, lice and even the afterbirth when their mares foaled. Cannibalism is reported by some observers, including Carpini, who tell of one siege where they had completely run out of supplies and were forced to kill one out

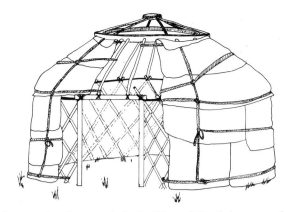

A *yurt*, the characteristic dwelling of the Asian nomads, made on a light wicker frame and covered in black felt; this is a Khirgiz type. A reconstruction by artist Heather Dockeray.

of every 10 men in their army for food. If this is true then the unlucky men were probably auxiliaries from conquered nations pressed into service. It is difficult to confirm cannibalism, as some chroniclers were no doubt carried away by their loathing and fear of the conquerors.

Other characteristics of the Mongols earn respect rather than disgust. For example, their eyesight was incredibly keen. Among the scarcely believable claims made for them was the assertion that on the wide plains of their homeland they could discern a man trying to hide behind a bush or a rock at four miles' distance, and that in the clear air of the dawn they could distinguish men from animals 18 miles away! Added to this was a good visual memory and a deep knowledge of climatic conditions, vegetation and water supply. No one but a pastoral nomad could have attained such heights of fieldcraft. He was taught to ride by his mother from the age of three, beginning by being tied to the horse's back. At four or five he was given his first bow and arrows, and from then on would spend much of his life with a bow in his hand, mounted on a horse's back, either waging war or hunting. On a campaign where speed was essential he would sleep in the saddle, and his speed was further increased by always taking with him between one and four remounts, which were ridden in turn for periods of up to 24 hours.

The Mongol horse was every bit as tough as its owner. It was, and still is, a short and stocky breed, 13 or 14 hands high. Its dense coat kept it warm in winter, and it was capable of some vast journeys. It is recorded that one Mongol on a single pony could cover 600 miles in nine days, and with the remount system mentioned above Genghis Khan's army covered 130 miles in two days in September 1221, with no breaks for food. In 1241 Subadai's army travelled 180 miles in three days through deep snow.

The Mongol horses would graze as they went along, rooting beneath the snow and eating leaves off trees, which accounts for Matthew Paris's comment that the 'powerful horses' ate the trees themselves. The horses were obedient to their riders, and were trained to provide a steady platform from which the rider could discharge his bow. The firm saddle, which weighed about 10lb and was high at the back and front, was rubbed with sheep's fat to prevent swelling in the rain. The stirrups, too, were solid, and slung from very short straps.

The Mongol's main weapon was the compound bow. It had a pull of 166lb, considerably more than an English longbow, and had a destructive range of 200 to 300 yards. Carpini states that the Mongols carried two bows, perhaps one long and one short, and two or three quivers holding 30 arrows each. Carpini distinguishes two sorts of arrows: light ones with small, sharp points for long-range shooting, and heavy ones with large, broad heads for close quarters. The heads, he says, were hardened by heating them until they were red-hot and then dipping them into salt water, a treatment which made them hard enough to pierce armour. The

Loading a pack-camel. Judging by the turbans, the artist may be attempting to reproduce Muslim captives.

The battle of Liegnitz. Note how the artist has illustrated the characteristic Mongol cap.

shafts of the arrows were fletched with eagle feathers.

Other weapons were used as well as the bow, their use depending on whether a warrior belonged to the heavy or light cavalry. The heavy cavalry carried a long lance fitted with a hook for pulling enemies from the saddle, and may have carried shields. Some illuminated manuscripts show small, round shields in use, but the most reliable sources emphasize that shields were only carried when the soldier was on foot. A large skin or wicker shield was employed while on sentry duty, and large tortoise-like ones for assaulting walls. Heavy cavalry might also carry a mace. Swords were in the form of light sabres imported or copied from the Muslim Turks. Light cavalrymen would have a sword and bows, and some would have javelins.

All Mongols on campaign would bear a light axe, a file for sharpening their arrowheads (fastened to the quiver), a horsehair lasso, a coil of stout rope, an awl, a needle and thread, a cooking pot variously described as iron or earthenware, and the two leather bottles already mentioned. A small tent was carried for each unit of 10 men. Each man would presumably have

had his own ration bag, and Carpini describes a large soft leather bag closed by a long thong to keep clothes and other equipment dry while crossing rivers. Carpini indicates how this bag was used. It was stuffed with clothes and the saddle was fixed securely to it. The bag was then tied to the horse's tail, and the rider would swim across holding on to the horse's bridle to guide it.

The armour worn by the Mongols is somewhat difficult to determine as all we have to work on are eye-witness accounts of equipment unfamiliar to the observer, and illustrations which may be misleading in view of their having been painted at a later date. Three materials are mentioned: leather, iron scales and chain-mail. Leather armour was made by joining various sections together to make a tough and flexible armour-plate, the leather having first been softened by boiling. The leather was weatherproofed by covering it with a crude lacquer made from pitch. Some authorities state that armour was only worn on the front of the body, others mention a back plate also. Carpini also observed iron armour, and gives a detailed description of how it was made. They took a number of thin plates of metal, a finger's-breadth wide and a hand's-breadth in length, and pierced eight holes in each plate. A series of such plates were bound together by leather thongs, and then several of these strips would be joined to make an armour-plate. This is in fact typical lamellar armour, as was worn in many oriental countries. Carpini noted that the armour was polished so brightly that one could see one's reflection in it.

These lamellar armour-plates were made up into suits. Several are illustrated in sources dating from later in our period, notably the illustrations to Raschid-al-Din's *World History*, painted about 1306, and the Japanese *Mongol Invasion Scroll*, painted about 1292. Allowing for the fact that both sources may derive some errors from their native traditions, there is good agreement between the two on points of detail, and it is possible to build up a picture of a typical armoured Mongol for at least the later, Kublai Khan, period. The armoured coat is long, reaching to well below the knees, but often showing the 'robe' beneath it. It opens all down the front, and is fastened as far down as the waist, no doubt for convenience in riding, and has short sleeves of armour-plate reaching to just above the elbow, reminiscent of the shoulder-plates on Japanese armour. In the Raschid-al-Din illustrations many warriors wear decorative surcoats over their armour, which tallies with the silken stuffs referred to above. The armour and surcoats shown on the Japanese scroll are very similar, the main difference in style being that on the Japanese scroll all the warriors look fiercer. Raschid-al-Din's are very stylized, and very clean!

Raschid-al-Din shows us a metal helmet with a central spike bending somewhat towards the rear. The Japanese scroll shows helmets ending in a round ball with a plume, and a very wide neck-guard covering the shoulders and coming round under the chin, while the Persian pictures show a smaller neck-guard.

The larger form of *yurt*, which were drawn on wagons behind an advancing army. In the distance *yurts* are being erected.

It seems reasonable to assume that this armour was being worn from at least the time of the European campaign onwards; prior to that period we have little to go on. No doubt some armour was worn, but it may have been simpler than the suits described above.

In winter the fur coats previously described would have been worn over the armour. Light cavalrymen may not have worn any armour at all; and as many authorities state that horse armour was worn as say that it was not. This, again, may indicate a distinction between light and heavy cavalry. Carpini describes leather lamellar horse armour made in five sections:

'. . . One on one side of the horse and one on the other, and these stretched from the tail to the head and are fastened to the saddle and behind

Just visible on the right of this damaged painting, a Mongol warrior is dressed in armour. (Courtesy of the Bildarchiv Preussischer Kulturbesitz)

the saddle on to its back and also on the neck; another section they put over its hindquarters where the ties of the two parts are fastened and in this last named piece they make a hole for the tail to come through; covering the breast is another section. All these pieces reach down as far as the knees or joints of the leg. On its forehead they put an iron plate which is tied to the afore-mentioned sections on each side of the neck.'

Friar William (c.1254) speaks of meeting two Mongols wearing chain-mail hauberks. The riders told him they obtained chain-mail from the Alans, who in turn had obtained it from the

Kubetsckis in the Caucasus. William adds that he saw armour made from iron plates, and iron caps, which they got from Persia, and states that the leather armour he saw was most unwieldy. Both he and Vincent de Beauvais state that only the important warriors wore armour, Vincent de Beauvais estimating it as one in ten.

Mongol Armies

The great achievement of Genghis Khan and his successors was making these rugged Mongol warriors into an army. It was a transformation performed so efficiently that to Western observers nothing could stand in its way. Robert of Spolato, a contemporary of the Mongol invasion of Europe, wrote that there was no people in the world who knew so well how to overcome an enemy in the open by skill at warfare.

It was believed by an earlier generation of historians that many Mongol victories were due to sheer weight of numbers. Careful examination of the evidence, however, shows that in the majority of cases the opposite was true, and that the Mongols were often greatly outnumbered, but that their superior mobility, best shown by their techniques of envelopment, led many European armies to believe that they were indeed surrounded by vastly superior forces.

Before discussing the actual size of Mongol armies it will be useful to examine the structure within such an army. The Mongol army was organized on the simple but effective lines of a decimal system. The smallest unit was a troop of 10, called an *arban*, under an officer called a *bagatur*. Ten *arbans* made a squadron of 100 called a *jagun*. Ten *jaguns* made a regiment of 1,000 called a *minghan*, and 10 *minghans* made the largest unit, the 10,000-strong *tumen*, which corresponds to a division. A typical Mongol army would consist of two or three *tumens*.

Transfer from one unit to another was strictly forbidden, and each man had his specific position and his particular job to do. It could well be a lifetime's service, as every able-bodied man between 14 and 60 years of age was liable for military duty.

The Mongol army was divided territorially into three main forces, and as the Mongols always

Mongol warriors in armour, from Raschid-al-Din's *World History*. (Courtesy of Edinburgh University Library)

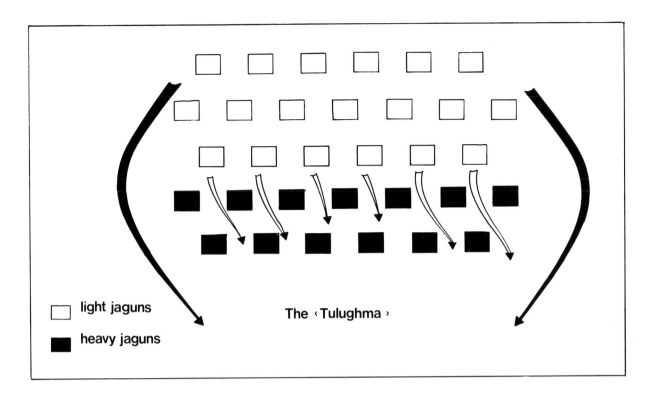

light jaguns

heavy jaguns

The ‹ Tulughma ›

pitched camp with their tents facing south the titles had actual physical significance. They were the Army of the Left Wing, or East (*Junghar*); the Army of the Right Wing, or West (*Baraunghar*); and the Army of the Centre (*Khol*). The army of the centre was in all probability the Imperial Guard, or *keshik*, for which the finest troops were selected. Sons of the commanders of *jaguns* and *minghans* were accepted automatically for the guard, while all other places were allocated on a competitive basis. All the army units were represented somewhere in the guard, and in common with all other parts of his army Genghis Khan made sure that all units were drawn from a mixture of families and tribes, thus ensuring that a unit's loyalty would be to the khan and not to a small faction. The guard, in fact, acted like a Mongol military academy. A fully-trained guardsman was reckoned fit to command a *tumen*, and had precedence over the commander of a *minghan*. The privileges the guard enjoyed compensated for their obligation to serve in peacetime as well as war. An extract from the rules laid down for the guards makes interesting reading:

'1. The commander of the shift on duty must himself stand night watch.

A diagram showing the *tulughma*, a manoeuvre whereby the light cavalry on the wings spread round to envelop the enemy while the centre was engaged. For full description see text.

'3. The first failure of a guardsman to appear on duty is to be punished with 30 strokes, a second failure with 70 strokes and a third failure with 37 strokes and expulsion from the guard . . .

'6. A member of the guard is to rank higher than any soldier of the line.'

The earliest record of the guard dates from 1203, when the day guard (*tunghaut*) consisted of 70 men, and the night guard (*kabtaut*) of 80 men. There were also about 1,500 others. In 1206, when Genghis Khan assumed complete power, the guard was increased to the size of a complete *tumen*. That part of the guard which was Genghis Khan's personal army (about one *minghan* in size) only took the field when he himself went to war.

When the Khan was present all marched under his orders, which were issued from beneath the *tuk*, his yak-tail standard. Yet although the Khan had supreme command, once the general orders had been given his subordinate commanders suffered little interference and needed little communication with higher authority. This basis of trust, founded on loyalty and experience, served the Mongols well. Skill at warfare counted far more highly than aristocratic birth, and where armies appear to have been commanded by princes the real decision-making was often carried out by a soldier risen from the ranks. Subadai is an excellent example. He commanded an army while he was still under 25 years old. As a mark of authority the commander of an army was given a great drum which was sounded only at his orders.

Marco Polo sums up the organization in these words:

'. . . His own orders have to be given to ten persons only . . . no one having to give orders to more than ten. And everyone in turn is responsible only to the officer immediately over him; and the discipline and order that comes of this method is marvellous, for they are a people very obedient to their chiefs . . .'

The overall number of troops in the Mongol army was often far less than that of their enemies. For example, in 1211 Genghis Khan commanded less than a quarter of the forces of his opponents, the Ch'in.

Because many Mongol campaigns were carried out far from home and over a long period it was difficult to reinforce a depleted army from Mongolia. A Chinese historian recalls having met some Mongol reinforcements in 1236, and they included boys of 13 or 14 years old; but as they had livestock with them they may only have been a supply column, ready to take their places in the ranks when old enough. The normal Mongol method of reinforcing armies was to absorb within them the forces of conquered nations. Sometimes they would be joined quite voluntarily by neighbouring tribes eager to share in the loot. China provided a large supply of impressed men, mainly infantry, and both China and Korea supplied large numbers for the invasion of Japan.

Raschid-al-Din states that at the time of the death of Genghis Khan in 1227 the total Mongol army numbered 123,000 men, organized as follows:

Left Wing	62,000
Right Wing	38,000

Guard:	
Imperial	1,000
Prince Juchi	4,000
Prince Chagadai	4,000
Prince Ogedei	4,000
Others	10,000

By the time Ogedei (1229–41) succeeded to the throne these numbers would have been increased considerably from the conquered territories.

It is worth repeating at this point that almost all of these troops were mounted, a very important factor to be borne in mind when Mongol warfare is discussed. This mobility was reflected in their dwellings, the *yurts*, of black felt on a collapsible wicker framework, light and easy to carry. Larger versions existed, but these were carried from place to place in one piece on heavy carts.

Mongol Warfare

'And ye shall understand that it is a great dread for to pursue the Tartars if they flee in battle . . .' wrote Sir John Mandeville, '. . . for in fleeing they shoot behind them and slay both men and horses. And when they will fight they will shock them together in a plump . . .'

In fact the 'great dread' of the Mongols began for an enemy long before the first arrow was fired. Before setting out on any campaign the Mongol command took pains to acquire as much information as possible about their intended victims. Scouts and spies made sure that the Khan knew of possible weak points in an enemy's defences, in particular of any rivalry between allies that could be turned to an invader's advantage, as well as vital information concerning roads, weather conditions, possible grazing grounds, etc. As they collected information the Mongols would begin to sow the seeds of dissension. The poor were told of liberation by the Mongols, while the rich were assured that commerce would be facilitated. Such psychological warfare would be stepped up after the *kuriltai*, the great council of

Mongol light cavalryman, Russia, c.1223

Mongols in winter coats with pack-camel, c.1211–60

Mongol heavy cavalryman, Liegnitz, 1241

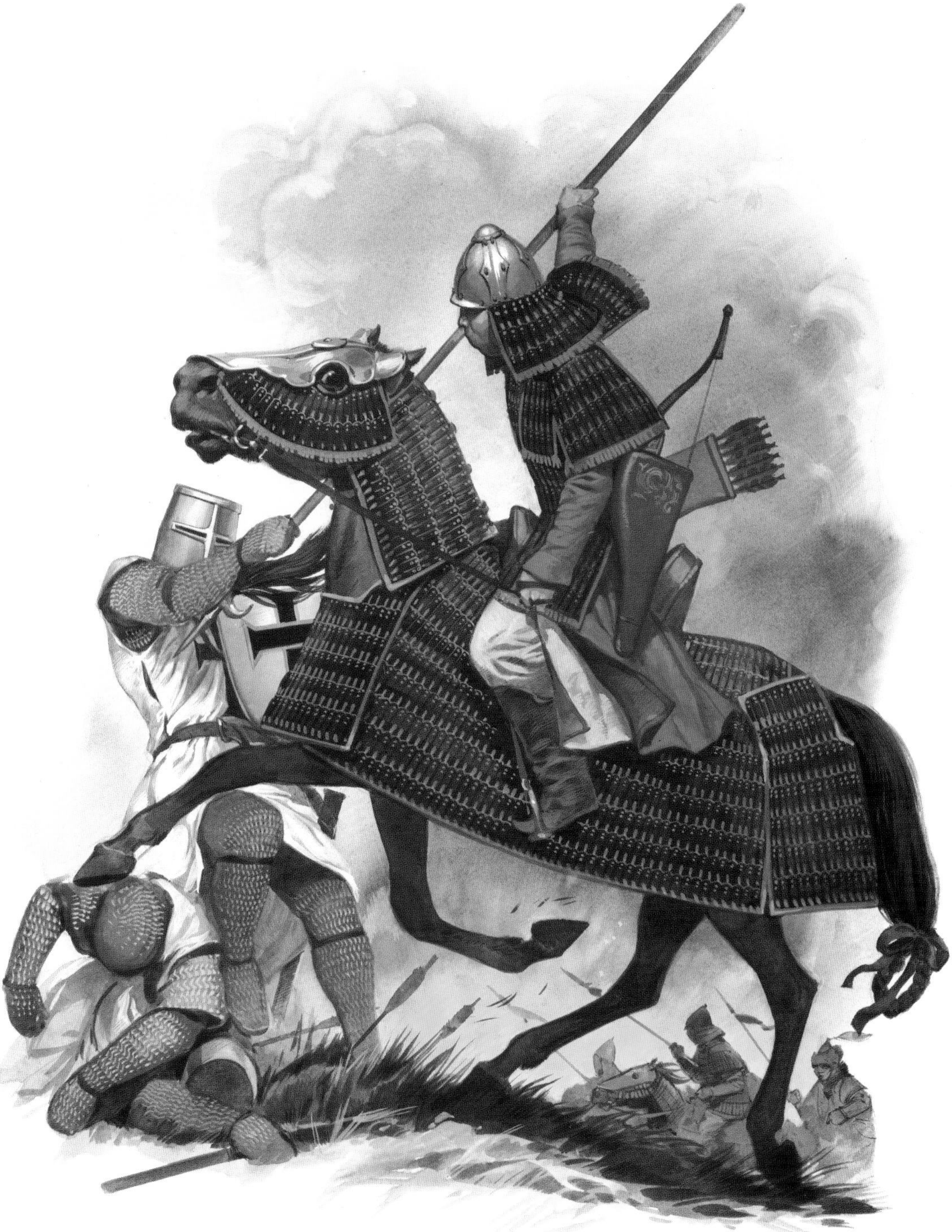

Mongol commander and naccara drummer, c.1240

D

Mongol camp, c.1220

Mongol camp, c.1210−60

F

Mongol heavy cavalry officer, China, c.1210—76

1. and 2. Korean auxiliaries, c.1280
3. Japanese samurai, c.1280

war at which the details of the campaign would be finalized, and would include the deliberate planting of rumours exaggerating the numbers of the invading army to be expected. There was no need to exaggerate the tales of Mongol cruelty and massacres. The facts alone spoke for themselves, and could produce a terror so stupefying that, as Ibn-al Athir records, a single Mongol horseman could enter a Persian village and begin killing people while no one dared to raise a hand to stop him. The chronicler added that he had heard that one Mongol took a man captive, but had no weapon with which to kill him. He told his prisoner to lie with his head on the ground without moving. The terror-stricken man did so, and remained there until the Mongol returned from fetching his sword and cut his head off.

At the *kuriltai* one factor to be decided was the season for the campaign to begin. Thus the Russian campaign was launched in the winter of 1237–38, against all military expectation, because the frozen rivers made the whole country like one vast, snow-covered Mongolia in which the winter-hardy Mongols would feel at home. Iraq was invaded in spring 1258 when heat and the danger of malaria were slight. At the *kuriltai* the numbers of the armies were fixed, and supplies were organized. To the Mongols the main sources of supply were the countries they planned to invade, but livestock was often driven on the hoof, and much equipment was carried by camels and pack-horses. It is a point to the Mongols' credit that when such plans were agreed upon they usually happened, and on time.

When the army was ready to move the officers would inspect their men's equipment, down to the very needle and thread carried for the repair of gear. (On the march, if a soldier dropped something the man riding behind was required to dismount and pick it up, lest he be punished.) Following a general review, the army would move off from its area of concentration.

The Mongols obeyed the dictum 'march divided, attack united'. They nearly always entered enemy territory in widely separated columns, between which communication was maintained. At every camp they established there were at least two horses kept saddled for sending messages. Smoke signals were also used. As a result the various parts of an invasion force could come together with amazing speed, their superior mobility giving them the same security that concentration gave to slower-moving armies. The advance of the column was so co-ordinated that the thrust of one produced a reaction to the advantage of the others.

The first Mongols to make contact with the enemy were the mobile scouts, operating up to 70 miles ahead of the main body. Similar screens operated on the flanks and the rear. Their constant supply of information gave the Mongol commanders full and up-to-date knowledge of enemy location, numbers, possible camp sites, etc. No one ever surprised a Mongol army.

Once the scouts had made contact with the enemy the main body would begin to extend its front over as wide an area as possible so as to overlap the enemy force. Meanwhile the lightly armed scouts tested the enemy's mettle by shooting at them and watching their reaction. If the body of enemy was small the vanguard itself might destroy them; otherwise they would retire to the main body, luring on the enemy as they went. At no time were the Mongols more dangerous than when they were apparently withdrawing, as we shall see.

Once the enemy army came into contact with the main body the deadly potential of Mongol tactical genius was revealed. The battle of Waterloo may not have been won on the playing-fields of Eton; but the battles of Mohi and Leignitz, to name but two, were victories conceived in the hunting grounds of the great khans. The hunt was the training for the Mongol warrior, and a lesson in tactics for his officers. In an operation of vast proportions the game was beaten into a huge, pre-selected reserve, and then the killing would begin. Whether the victims of the chase were enemy soldiers or wild animals, the whole operation was carried out methodically and ruthlessly.

Once the enemy were prepared for action the Mongol army took up its battle formation. The standard formation consisted of five ranks, each *jagun* being separated by wide intervals. The two front ranks consisted of heavy cavalry armed with lances, maces and swords, and probably with armoured horses too. The remaining three ranks were light cavalry with little or no armour and armed with bows and javelins. When battle began the light cavalry advanced through the gaps in the heavy *jaguns* and poured a devastating volley of arrows and javelins into the enemy ranks. At the same time either or both the wings of light cavalry began an encircling movement to take the enemy in the flank or in the rear, a tactic known as the *tulughma*, or 'standard sweep'. If any light troops were forced back by an enemy's determination they calmly withdrew, shooting as they went, and their place was taken by other units. Very soon the enemy would become disorganized, at which point a charge by the heavy cavalry would be ordered.

What is amazing about the battle movements so far described is that they were all carried out in perfect, eerie silence, the instructions to move being given by the raising and lowering of black and white flags, or at night by lanterns. At the moment of the charge all the Mongols followed the pounding of the great *naccara*, the war drums carried on the back of a camel. Once the drums began the Mongols surged forward, screaming wildly, the light cavalry following the heavy, and usually accompanied by a simultaneous surprise

assault on flank or rear. The Mongol cunning extended to never quite surrounding an enemy, which would have given him an opportunity to fight to the last man. Instead a way of escape was always left, through which the terrified enemy would be allowed to flee, to be cut down in the open at the Mongols' leisure.

No army knew better than the Mongols the importance of pursuit. A beaten enemy would be harassed for days, and all the surrounding countryside devastated. After the defeat of the Mamluks at Salamiyet in 1299 Mongol soldiers were seen as far south as Gaza, over 300 miles from the scene of battle.

The rôle of the guard in such battles was often that of an élite force held in reserve either to strike the decisive blow or to repulse a strong enemy countercharge, as was the case at the battle of Nilab in 1221.

The use of a fake retreat has already been noted. It was often accompanied by other tricks designed to confuse the enemy, such as stirring up dust clouds as the wings advanced. Even after the trick of retreating became well known it still proved effective. If necessary it was continued for days, for example Jebe and Subadai's nine-day retreat in May 1222. Over this space of time the better-mounted troops of the Prince of Galich and his Kipchak allies had moved far ahead of the Russians. The Mongols had all the while

Mongol warriors in battle, from Raschid-al-Din's *World History*. (Courtesy of Edinburgh University Library)

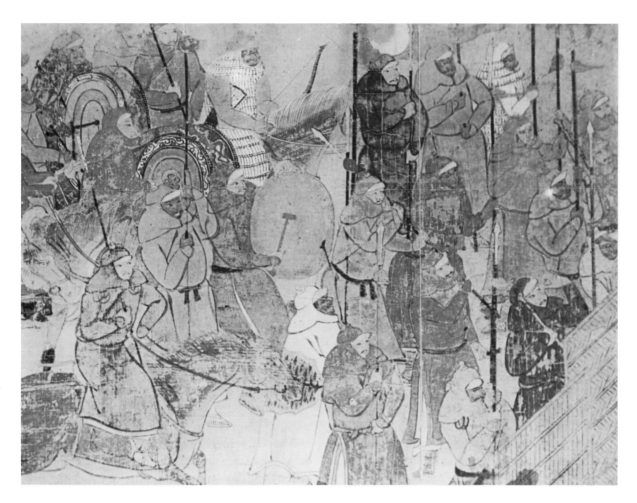

been spreading round their flanks, and were able to launch a crushing attack on to the Kipchak army before the slower-moving contingent could come to their aid. They in turn were attacked so swiftly that they were surrounded and soon surrendered.

The Mongol remount system enabled a feigned retreat to be carried out with the minimum discomfort to horse and rider, a fact which Carpini noted in his recommendations after his journey. Carpini knew their tricks well. 'Even if the Tartars retreat,' he wrote, 'our men ought not to separate from each other or be split up, for the Tartars pretend to withdraw in order to divide an enemy.' Carpini's other suggestions show his understanding of Mongol warfare. He recommends crossbows, 'of which they are much afraid', and lances with a hook to drag the Mongols off their saddles, 'for they fall off easily'. Breast plates, he added, should be of double thickness.

Another ruse used by the Mongols was that of

Mongol warriors during the attempted invasion of Japan. Two are armoured. From the *Mongol Invasion Scroll*.

stuffed dummies mounted on the spare horses to indicate a larger force. Carpini refers to this in connection with the Mongol commanders, who, he says, sat surrounded by dummy warriors. He noted that the commanders did not actually fight in the battle, but stayed at a distance, from where they could control the whole conduct of operations.

Mongol field warfare was therefore an almost perfect combination of firepower, shock tactics and mobility. The moves themselves, built on a sound framework of experience, training and discipline, were performed like clockwork. Strategy seems to have been innately understood, and their morale was unquestionable. They believed themselves to be invincible, and most of the vanquished believed it too, regarding them as a visitation from heaven and a punishment for sin. The word 'Tartar', used by the chroniclers, comes partly from confusion with a tribe called the Tatars, but mainly from identifying the Mongols as '. . . an immense horde of that detestable race of Satan . . . like demons loosed from Tartarus'—Tartarus meaning Hell.

So the Mongol art of warfare provides a lesson by demonstrating that cavalry do not necessarily have to rest on a stable infantry base. However, when conditions changed the Mongols had to alter their ideas, so before examining the European campaign, and seeing how it illustrates the points discussed above, let us examine the one area of warfare where the Mongols were at first less than successful.

Mongol Sieges

In their early campaigns the Mongols had one Achilles' heel: the reduction of walled towns and cities. The Japanese were to reveal another in later years, namely amphibious warfare; but at first the conduct of siege operations seems to have

Armoured Mongol warriors in action. A further scene from Raschid-al-Din's *World History*. (Courtesy of Edinburgh University Library)

caused the Mongols some confusion, not only over how to conduct a siege, but also over what to do with the city once it had fallen.

It was to the Mongols' advantage that they fully realized their technological limitations right from the start, and in all their campaigns it is evident that the Mongols preferred to deal with the field forces of their enemies before penetrating very far into hostile territory. If they were forced to attack fortified positions then they always tried to leave the most heavily defended ones to the last. For any nation at this period in history sieges were long and costly undertakings, and quite different exercises from the dramatic swoops that the Mongols had perfected. Their lack of expertise in these matters was shown dramatically in 1209 when Genghis Khan besieged the Hsi-Hsia fortress of Chung-hsiung. The Mongols very cleverly built a dyke to flood the fortress, but instead succeeded in flooding their own camp. Surprisingly enough the Hsi-Hsia surrendered anyway, no doubt expecting that a natural soldier like Genghis Khan would get it right eventually.

The Mongols' wisest move was to take into their service Chinese, and later Muslim, siege experts. These were employed as early as 1211, and from this time on Chinese siege engines were used regularly.

To Western eyes accustomed to medieval trebuchets worked on a counterpoise system, the Chinese siege catapults appear very strange.

They worked on a lever principle, whereby several levers (up to 10) were fastened together and kept in balance on a mount. At one end was a receptacle for the projectile, while at the other end were numerous ropes which were simply pulled, flinging the missile into the air. The efficiency of such weapons of course depended on the number of men to pull the ropes, ranging from a single-lever catapult fired by 20 men pulling two ropes each, to the largest with a pulling crew of 250 on 125 ropes, firing a 90lb stone. The ranges claimed for early catapults are not very great; but in a work written in the 12th century the author claims that vast improvements had been made, and quotes ranges for a single-lever catapult of between 250 and 270 paces, with a smaller operating crew of 10 to 15 men. For 'far-reaching' catapults he gives 350 paces as the maximum effective range, but it is difficult to see exactly how the pulling crew would be arranged so as to get an efficient tug on the ropes without getting in each other's way.

The wood used for such weapons was oak, and the ropes were made from hemp and leather twisted together — because if the weather was fine, leather would shrink and hemp distend, while in rainy weather leather becomes soft and hemp shrinks. Clay balls are also recommended for a siege as they burst on impact and cannot there-

A Chinese painting depicting Mongol horsemen. The illustration is highly stylized.

fore be fired back at you.

The use of Muslim versions of siege engines, in particular the trebuchet, is noted for the siege of Hsiang-yang, a Sung city that held out for five years against Kublai Khan. In 1273 he received trebuchets from his cousin the Il-khan of Persia. The noise of these machines, and the crash of the missile as it broke through everything in its fall, caused great alarm in the garrison. The massive engines hurled 166lb rocks with such force that they penetrated the beaten clay walls to a depth of seven or eight feet.

The weapons used by and against the Mongols must have been fairly efficient, because we read that at the siege of Kai-fung in 1232 Subadai had his engineers throw quarters of millstones, which smashed the battlements and watchtowers on the ramparts, and even the large timbers of houses in the city. During a siege in 1220 the engineers had no stones so cut logs of wood from mulberry trees, hardening them by soaking in water.

The Sung Chinese had a crossbow artillery, adapted by the Mongols, in which up to three single crossbows were combined in one. They were mounted on a wooden structure and could only be moved with difficulty because they were so heavy. They were cocked by winding a wheel and needed large numbers of men to operate them. A triple crossbow needed as many as 100 crewmen. Effective range was about 200 yards.

Of the projectiles fired from catapults none are more interesting than those which involved gunpowder or some other incendiary material. In 1232 the Chi'tan, defending the city of Lo-yang against the Mongols, fired a 'thunder-bomb' (*chen t'ien lei*) from a catapult. This was an iron vessel filled with gunpowder, fitted with a fuse the lighting of which automatically fired the catapult. It exploded with a great noise. There is a well-known section of the Japanese *Mongol Invasion Scroll* which shows a similar weapon exploding in front of a horseman.

At the siege of Baghdad in 1258 the Mongols used fire arrows, and naphtha pots fired from catapults. The naphtha pots were probably 'Greek Fire', compounded of a mixture of naphtha and quicklime. Several different types of incendiary were known to the Sung, including

oil-soaked hemp or cotton. By 1273 at least, methods had been found of neutralizing the effects of incendiary attacks. One method was to make ropes from rice straw, about four inches thick, and lay them side by side on top of a building, covering the whole with clay. A recipe for a gas bomb was already known in the 11th century. Called a 'poison-and-smoke ball' (*tu-yao yen ch'iu*), it weighed 5lb and included in its composition sulphur, nitre, aconite, oil, powdered charcoal, resin and wax.

The outstanding feature of Mongol siegecraft was not the size and variety of weapons used, but the numbers employed and the ruthless use made of captives to operate them. At the siege of Nishapur in 1221 the Mongols were faced with defences which included 3,000 heavy javelin throwers and 500 heavy catapults mounted on the walls. In response the Mongols forced their captives, including many from neighbouring cities recently conquered, to set up Mongol siegeworks under the fire from Nishapur. Some 3,000 'ballistae' (probably multiple crossbows) were erected, and 3,700 catapults of various design for throwing rocks or naphtha compound. Besides this, 4,000 scaling ladders were made and 2,500 loads of rock brought down from the near-

A Mongol firebomb explodes in front of a Japanese samurai. Note also the detailed illustration of Mongol weapons. From the *Mongol Invasion Scroll*.

by mountains. Not content with their use as draught beasts, the Mongols forced the captives to lead the assault parties, since losses among them meant nothing to their cruel masters. Such techniques were often used against forts, and sometimes even in field battles.

In spite of all the Chinese and Muslim expertise acquired by the Mongols, it is apparent that such static siege warfare was not to their liking. If possible a blockading force would be detached from the main body until, hopefully, the enemy field forces had been defeated and resistance by a garrison therefore became pointless. It is more than likely that one reason for the horrific slaughter of defeated garrisons, and sometimes of entire cities, was to intimidate other local garrisons into surrendering so that the Mongols did not have to suffer the tiresome business of conducting a siege.

Garrisoning a conquered area was another field in which the Mongols lacked expertise. During their conquest of north China several cities had to be recaptured two or three times, so eventually the Mongol High Command assigned auxiliaries to such duties.

In conclusion we may note what appears to be a significant advance in warfare associated with the Mongols, namely a very primitive form of cannon. In 1259 Chinese technicians produced a 'fire-lance' (*huo-ch'iang*). Gunpowder was exploded in a bamboo tube to discharge a cluster of pellets a distance of 250 yards. It is also interesting to note the Mongol use of suffocating fumes produced by burning reeds at the battle of Liegnitz in 1241.

The Mongols in Russia and Europe

There is no better way of illustrating the various facets of Mongol warfare than to study the classic expedition against Russia and Eastern Europe, the most audacious of the four campaigns considered at the memorable *kuriltai* of 1235. Prince Juchi's second son Batu was appointed to lead the army, with Subadai—the wily old general who had been one of Genghis Khan's original 'Four Hounds'—as his chief-of-staff. In fact Subadai probably had overall command, as many of the bold strategic decisions bear his hallmark.

Information suggested that the wisest course of action would be to defeat the Bulgars and Kipchaks first, and thus safeguard the Mongol lines

of communication along the Volga and the Don. This operation began in 1236, Mongke taking on the Kipchaks, and Batu and Subadai the Bulgars. By autumn 1237 their defeat was complete, and the Mongol army crossed the Volga to attack Russia in the winter of 1237, a decision that no one but a Mongol could have taken. They also judged rightly, no doubt on the basis of accurate intelligence reports, that the Russians would be unprepared. The Russians were, not only because of the weather, but also in their assumption that once the campaign had begun the Mongols would take far longer to crush the Bulgars.

The strongest point in eastern Russia was the fortified city of Vladimir, whose garrison was under the command of the Grand Duke Yuri II. This the Mongols chose to avoid, and instead performed an outflanking movement by assaulting Riazan on the middle of the River Oka. Riazan was submitted to a five-day bombardment by catapults from a few hundred yards' range, and was finally stormed on 21 December 1237. 'No eye remained open to weep for the dead,' wrote one chronicler. 'Some were impaled, or had nails or splinters of wood driven under their finger-nails. Priests were roasted alive, and nuns and maidens ravished in the churches before their relatives.'

The next town to fall was the then minor settlement of Moscow. Vladimir was now completely outflanked. In panic Grand Duke Yuri fled north to take up headquarters on the River Sit, leaving Vladimir with a force much depleted and divided. Subadai sent the Mongol vanguard on northwards to Sit, and commenced a brief six-day siege of the once-strong Vladimir, ending on 8 February 1238, when, according to the chronicler, 'stones fell like rain'. With Vladimir destroyed the River Sit positions could be attacked at leisure, and Grand Duke Yuri soon met his death.

The Mongols accordingly headed for Novgorod, but when only 65 miles away from this rich prize they stopped, and wheeled away to the south. Spring was on its way, with the prospect of

A highly detailed illustration of the siege of a town, from the Saray Album. (Courtesy of the Bildarchiv Preussischer Kulturbesitz)

a thaw which would make the roads impassable, so the army headed for the Don basin, there to rest before commencing a fresh onslaught. On their way they bypassed all cities except Kozelsk, in Kaluga, which suffered a seven-week siege.

The first phase of the Russian campaign was over. During 1239 there was little activity. Many of the surviving Kipchaks and Polovtsy nomads fled to Hungary, where they were given refuge by King Bela IV on condition that they became Christian. They were the first of several migrations to Hungary that were to give such a splendid pretext for attacking that country in the years to come.

In 1240 the Mongols set off again and captured Chernigov, then turned on Kiev. Kiev was a magnificent city, proud and defiant of the Mongols, as its inhabitants showed by executing the Mongol emissaries sent to demand their surrender. Batu himself is supposed to have been spellbound by the size and beauty of the city, but aesthetic considerations did not prevent him from commencing a fierce attack. One chronicler claimed that the vast quantities of arrows fired into the city obscured the light, and '. . . the squeaking of wagons, bellowing of camels, sounds of trumpets and organs, neighing of horses and cries and sobs of innumerable multitudes of people made it impossible to hear one another in the city.' Kiev fell on 6 December 1240, with much slaughter. When Carpini saw the ruins of the city six years later he could even then observe 'countless skulls and bones of dead men'. 'The inhabitants greeted us', he wrote, 'as if we were risen from the dead.'

(There is a Russian legend concerning the fall of Kiev. A certain holy warrior called Mikhailik is supposed to have picked up the golden gates of the city 'like a sheaf of holy corn' on his spear point, riding invisibly through the Mongol host to Constantinople.)

The next target was Hungary. Its wide grassy plains, protected to the north-east by the Carpathian Mountains, offered an excellent base for future attacks on western Europe. The court of King Bela had also provided a haven for several Russian princes who had fled after the fall of Kiev. The attack was planned with meticulous precision on a scale that was impressive even by

Mongol standards. The main thrust was to be delivered from the point of concentration (between the headwaters of the Vistula and Halicz) towards Pest, the Mongol army penetrating the passes of the Carpathians in the dead of winter. To cover the vulnerable right flank Kaidu was entrusted with a campaign which virtually amounted to an invasion of Poland, and produced results equally as devastating as the main campaign.

Turning first to the attack on Poland we note, as the Mongols clearly did, the divisions among the defenders of the country. One such was Boleslav 'the Chaste', ruler of Cracow and Sandomir, who became the first of the Polish sovereigns to be defeated by the Mongols; he retired from Sandomir to Cracow in January 1241, the Mongols having crossed the frozen Vistula. He soon abandoned Cracow as well, which the Mongols entered, ironically, on Palm Sunday, 24 March 1241. They crossed the Oder near Ratebor by means of rafts or by swimming, and divided the army into two. Half of the Mongol army proceeded to ravage Greater Poland, while the other half advanced on Breslau.

The town was soon abandoned, but the citadel of Breslau appeared impregnable, so the Mongols bypassed it to attack the army of Silesia at Liegnitz. (Legend adds a romantic note to this decision, claiming that the prayers of the Prior of the Dominican convent of St Adelbert caused a light from heaven to fall on to his head, which dazzled and alarmed the invaders.)

The army of Silesia was commanded by the Silesian ruler Henry II 'the Pious'. As he rode out to do battle with the Mongols he was nearly struck by a stone that fell from the roof of St Mary's church, an accident which was regarded as a very bad omen. His force, augmented by numerous allies, drew up to face the Mongols at Liegnitz. Henry divided his army into four. The first contingent consisted of picked troops from Silesia and Greater Poland, together with some mercenaries, under Henry himself. The second was an army of Teutonic knights, clad in their mantles of white with black crosses, under their Grand Master. The third was a Polish contingent, and the fourth an army of 'gold digging peasants from Silesia'.

The Mongols confused Henry's army by burning reeds which gave off a thick, foul-smelling smoke. Above the cloud, which concealed the Mongol movements, the Poles could see the *tuk* standard, which in this case consisted of the crossed bones of a sheep and long black yak-tails. The Mongol light cavalry poured showers of arrows into the ranks, and then withdrew to be pursued by the Teutonic knights and the third, Polish, contingent. The rest of the battle followed the usual Mongol pattern, leaving Henry the Pious surrounded, with just four followers. These were cut down when Henry's horse gave way, and Henry, badly wounded in the armpit, was seized by the Mongols and decapitated. His headless and naked body was recognized later by his wife because of the six toes he bore on his left foot.

Decisive though the victory of Liegnitz may have been, it was not the main objective of the Mongol advance. The target was still Hungary, and while Kaidu had been ravaging Poland four separate columns of Mongols had been crossing the Carpathians to assemble at Pest. Baidar led the northernmost penetration, Batu went through Galicia, Kuyuk through Moldavia and Transylvania, and Subadai in a sweep to the south through the Mehedia Pass. Gathering at Pest, the combined army set in motion a large-scale fake retreat which lasted for nine days, and drew on King Bela and his allies to the River Sajo.

The Mongols crossed the river by the bridge near to the village of Mohi, and made camp on the rising ground separated from the river by swampy land. To frustrate reconnaissance from the river side they concealed their camp with brushwood. The Hungarians pitched camp on the western bank, leaving the river between them and the Mongols, but they pitched their tents rather too close together for safety, making the ropes holding them to the ground an obstacle to movement. Batu noted their ill-chosen disposition, and likened them to 'cattle pent up in a narrow stable'.

The Mongols attacked by night while the Hungarians were still sleeping. Supported by the fire of catapults, Batu led an attack on the bridge, which the Hungarians had guarded with only 1,000 men. Leading the defence of the bridge was

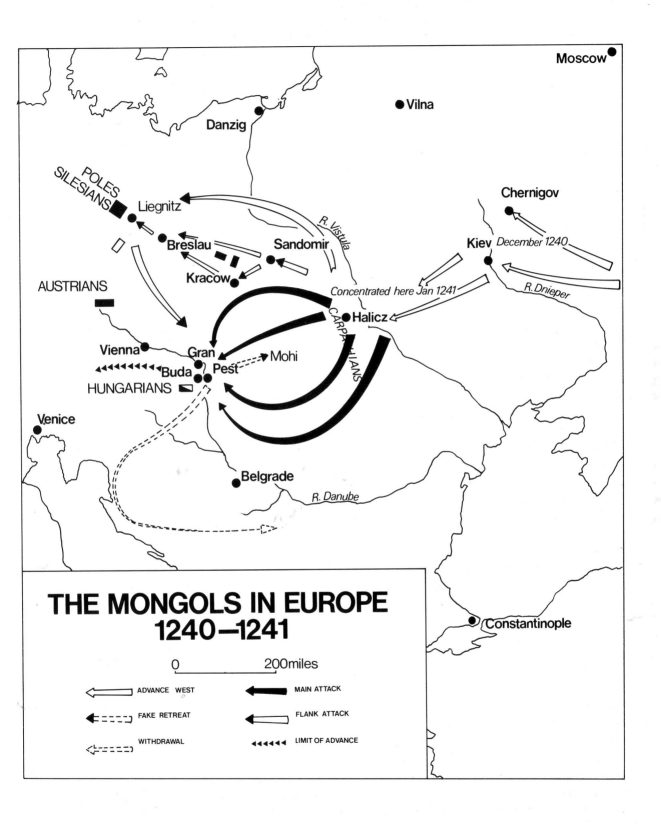

Moscow

Vilna

Danzig

POLES
SILESIANS
Liegnitz

R. Vistula

Breslau
Sandomir
Kracow

AUSTRIANS

Chernigov

Kiev *December 1240*

Concentrated here Jan 1241

R. Dnieper

CARPATHIANS

Halicz

Vienna
Gran
Mohi
Buda Pest
HUNGARIANS

Venice

Belgrade

R. Danube

Constantinople

THE MONGOLS IN EUROPE
1240–1241

0   200 miles

ADVANCE WEST   MAIN ATTACK

FAKE RETREAT   FLANK ATTACK

WITHDRAWAL   LIMIT OF ADVANCE

The Japanese hero Suenaga boards a Mongol ship, from the *Mongol Invasion Scroll*.

a certain King Koloman of the Ruthenians, the Duke of Slavonika, who in the first onslaught hurled a Mongol officer, with his horse and weapons, off the bridge and into the river. Eventually the hail of Mongol arrows forced him to return to camp, whence he returned with augmented forces and fought until he and Archbishop Ugolin retired wounded, leaving a contingent of the Knights Templar still fighting.

Meanwhile Subadai had forded the river upstream and surprised the Hungarians in the flank. In the Hungarian camp all was confusion as the terrified knights tripped over the tent ropes in their eagerness to flee. The Mongols calmly let them run through their ranks, to be hunted down by the light cavalry afterwards. A chronicler later noted that the land was strewn with corpses for a two-day journey.

With King Bela in flight Pest was open to the Mongols, and on entering the city it was burned to the ground. The battle of Mohi was a victory every bit as crushing as Liegnitz, and by strange coincidence was achieved on the same day, 9 April 1241.

During the summer of 1241 the Mongols forced the Hungarian peasants to sow and reap for them, and when winter came again they began their advance on Austria by crossing the frozen Danube to attack Gran. By February 1242 they were on their way to Vienna.

It is interesting to speculate what might have happened had the news not reached them of the death of Ogedei Khan, requiring them to return to choose a successor. With one accord the Mongols sadly withdrew, as it turned out never to return, and the great campaign of 1237–42 made the Mongols, as far as Europe was concerned, the Last of the Barbarians.

The Plates

A: Mongol light cavalryman, Russia, c.1223
A scene during the long pursuit which followed the battle of the River Khalka, perhaps: a Russian straggler hiding under a river bank has been picked off by a Mongol rider. The Mongol's robe, looted during the campaign against the Khwarizm Empire, is worn over a heavy coat; the wide-brimmed hat is lined with fur. The

costume is taken from a painting in the Saray Album in Istanbul. On his pony can be seen a coil of rope, an axe, and a leather bottle of milk curds. The Russian's armour is taken from specimens in the Kremlin armouries.

B: Mongols in winter coats with pack-camel, c.1211–60

The well-to-do Mongol in the foreground with the long spear is wearing two fur coats one on top of the other with the fur sides reversed; they could be of wolf, fox or even Russian bearskin. The conical hat is turned down against the cold. Men of lower status and wealth, such as the camel-hand, wore coats of dog or pony skin. The Bactrian camel was a useful beast of burden for the Mongols, and could carry a weight of up to 300lb. Six or seven layers of felt were placed in front of, between and behind the humps to give a level surface for the wooden saddle boards.

C: Mongol heavy cavalryman, Liegnitz, 1241

The leather lamellar armour, waterproofed with black pitch, is based on Carpini's description and on guide-lines given by H. R. Robinson in his *Oriental Armour*. The helmet, based on an illustrated Tibetan example, accords well with descriptions of those worn by the Mongols: the bowl is made from eight sections laced together with doeskin, and the peak is also laced in place. The horse armour is described by Carpini; its method of assembly accords well with stylized but recognizable Islamic paintings of perhaps half a century later. The spearhead is fitted with a hook and a yak-tail plume. The enemy knights wear the surcoat of the Teutonic Order.

D: Mongol commander and naccara drummer, c.1240

A Mongol commander about to launch his *tumen* against a Russian army, having already benefited from the spoils of conquest. He rides a well-bred Persian pony, harnessed in Mongol style but with a Persian hair tassel. The saddle cloth with a circular edge is from Chinese sources. The lamellar armour follows Carpini and Robinson: it is brightly burnished. The helmet, of laced construction, is from the same source; the mace is from Islamic paintings. For the *naccara* drummer we follow an old illustration reproduced in Col.

**A map of the battle of Mohi, where the Mongols defeated King Bela IV of Hungary. (Based on an original in Spruner-Menke's *Handatlas fur die Geschischte des Mittlapters.)*

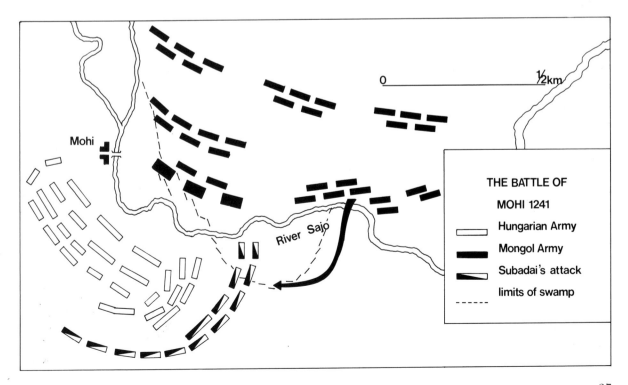

Yule's *Marco Polo*, which shows the long tassels on the drum cradles. The mail shirt is from Friar William of Rubruck's description; its use by a drummer is speculative, but logical, given the importance of this soldier in an army which manoeuvred on signals in a disciplined manner, and given his unavoidably exposed position.

E: Mongol camp, c.1220
A typical Mongol mounted archer wearing a long coat unadorned by either armour or robes; note how it fastens across the breast from left to right. The gear slung around the saddle, and the quiver, are taken from contemporary illustrations, as is the method of 'shackling' prisoners in the field. The child in the foreground, dressed exactly like an adult, has a pet *illik* or roe deer fawn. The women in the background are erecting a *yurt*, in this case of lime-washed felt.

F: Mongol camp, c.1210–60
The successful huntsman on the right has

abandoned his fur cap in the heat of summer for the type of headband described in Howorth's *History of the Mongols*. Falconry has always been, and remains today, a popular Mongol pastime. The sitting Mongol displays the elaborate hairstyle described in the body of the text. The gear is from various central Asian sources; the cooking pot and wind-break screens are from *The Story of Wen Chi*, a 12th-century source in the Museum of Fine Arts, Boston. Note rolled-up door-curtain of the *yurt*; and very baggy trousers tucked into boots.

G: Mongol heavy cavalry officer, China, c.1210–76
The source of both main figures in this scene of the Mongols assaulting a Chinese city is Raschid-al-Din; and here the comments in the text on the uncertain influence of stylized national artistic conventions on our view of remote peoples and periods apply with full force. The standing figure in the foreground is dressed in a style frequently depicted by Raschid-al-Din's artist, with a sleeveless robe exposing the shoulder-guards of a lamellar armour worn beneath it. The helmet is very 'Persian' in appearance; the broad section

An odd Westernised view of a Mongol warrior, in characteristic cap, under the feet of the effigy of Henry the Pious.

of 'turn-up' at the base of the skull is very commonly shown in Raschid-al-Din, but its significance is unknown. One is tempted to compare it with the turned-up brim sections of Mongol caps . . . to go further is pure speculation. The cheetah's tail on the quiver is found in several illustrations, and was perhaps used for wiping clean retrieved arrows.

The mounted Mongol wears a style of coat apparently different from that worn by the standing officer. Raschid-al-Din's artist consistently gives the impression that no armour is worn beneath it, and we have followed this convention. The reader will find further comment on the curiously inefficient-looking catapult in the body of the text. The reconstruction here is based on the most reliable available evidence, and it seems clear that propulsion was by 'prisoner-power', although the thrust obtainable by this method would seem very limited. Dr Joseph Needham (*Times Literary Supplement*, 11 January 1980) states that the more familiar counter-weighted trebuchet was no more than an Arabic improvement on this Chinese model.

A map of the Mongol campaign against Russia.

H1 and H2: Korean auxiliaries, c.1280

These figures, taken from the Japanese *Mongol Invasion Scroll*, represent auxiliaries pressed into Mongol service for the ill-fated Japanese expedition. They wear long, stitched fabric coats; weapons are the normal Mongol bow, and spears and swords. Note the large wickerwork shield on a bamboo frame.

H3: Japanese samurai, c.1280

The samurai is based on figures in the *Mongol Invasion Scroll*, and extant specimens of Japanese armour of the period. Note the right sleeve left free of armour for ease in drawing a bow, and the spare bowstring reel carried at the waist. (See also *The Samurai*, by the present author, published by Osprey.)

Notes sur les planches en couleur

A Costume mongol comprenant une robe asiatique pillée, portée par dessus un manteau épais dessiné d'après un tableau dans l'Album Saray à Istanbul. Armure russe d'après des exemples au Kremlin. Notez la corde, la hache et le flacon en cuir suspendu à la selle.

B Les Mongols portaient souvent deux manteaux de fourrure, celui de dessous était porté avec le côté fourrure à même le corps et celui de dessus avec le côté fourrure à l'extérieur. Les hommes riches portaient des manteaux de loup, de renard ou d'ours; les guerriers plus humbles utilisaient des peaux de chien ou de poney. Le chameau était la bête de somme habituelle parmi les Mongols.

C Armure lamellaire en cuir, rendue étanche par l'application d'une couche de brai noir, illustrée d'après la description de Carpini et d'après des modèles asiatiques survivants illustrés dans le livre *Oriental Armour* de H.R. Robinson. Le casque, composé de sections lacées, est dessiné d'après un modèle tibétain qui existe toujours. La lance est munie d'un crochet et sa tête est garnie d'une queue de yack en guise de plumet.

D Le dessin de l'armure et de la sellerie du commandant est tiré de diverses sources d'information sur l'Asie, du livre de Robinson, ansi que de tableaux chinois et persans. Le tambour *naccara* porte une cotte de mailles—ce qui est logique, étant donné sa position exposée sur le champ de bataille; la cotte de mailles est dessinée d'après la description de Carpini.

E Archer-chevalier mongol typique, vêtu du costume quotidien ordinaire; notez la méthode de lier les prisonniers et le *yurt* à l'arrière-plan.

F Notez le détail de la coiffure. Les Mongols ont toujours aimé la fauconnerie. Les divers articles d'équipment et le matériel de camping sont dessinés d'après des illustrations asiatiques.

G Dessins de costumes dont la conception est imaginée en grande partie d'après 'L'Histoire du Monde' de Raschid-al-Din. Le lance-pierres portatif est manipulé par des cordes tirées par des prisonniers: ceci parait inefficace comme méthode, mais les sources d'information à notre disposition sont parmi les meilleures possibles.

H Le dessin des auxiliaires coréens, recrutés au service des Mongols pour la malheureuse expédition japonaise, est tiré du parchemin japonais intitulé 'L'Invasion Mongole'; notez les manteaux de tissus épais cousu et le grand bouclier en vannerie et bambou. Le dessin du samurai est tiré du même document et ses armures sont copiées de celles de la même période qui survivent à ce jour.

Farbtafeln

A Ein Mongolenkostüm eines erbeuteten asiatischen Gewands über einem schweren Mantel, von einem Gemälde im Saray Album, Istanbul, entnommen. Russische Rüstung, einem Muster im Kremel entnommen. Bemerke das Seil, die Axt und die Lederflasche, die am Sattel befestigt sind.

B Mongolen trugen oftmals zwei Fellmäntel, den inneren mit dem Fell dem Körper zugewandt und den äusseren mit dem Fell nach aussen. Reiche Männer trugen Mantel aus Wolf- Fuchs- oder Bärenfell; bescheidenere Krieger benutzten Hund- oder Ponyfell. Das Bactrian Kamel war das normale Lasttier unter Mongolen.

C Lederne lamellenartige Rüstung, mit Pech wasserundurchlässig gemacht, gemalt nach Carpini's Beschreibung und von erhaltenen asiatischen Mustern, dargestellt in H.R. Robinson's *Oriental Armour*. Der Helm, aus zusammengeschnürten Einzelteilen, ist auf einem erhaltenen tibetanischem Muster basiert. Die Lanze hat einen Haken und die Quaste eines Yakschwanzes am Kopf befestigt.

D Die Rüstung und das Sattelzeug des Kommandeurs sind von verschiedenen asiatischen Quellen entnommen, besonders von Robinson's Buch sowie chinesischen und persischen Gemälden. Der *naccara* Trommler trägt Kettenpanzerrüstung—eine logische Annahme, bedenkt man seine freistehende Position im Kampf; die Rüstung ist Carpini's Beschreibung entnommen.

E Typischer mongolischer Reiter-Bogenschütze im normalen Alltagskostüm; bemerke die Art und Weise die Gefangenen zu binden; und *yurt* im Hintergrund.

F Bemerke die Einzelheiten der Frisur. Falkenjagd war bei den Mongolen immer beliebt gewesen. Die verschiedenen Ausrüstungsgegenstände und die Campierausrüstung wurden asiatischen Darstellungen entnommen.

G Spekulative Rekonstruktion des Kostümes hauptsachlich basiert auf der 'Geschichte der Welt' des Raschid-al-Din. Das tragbare Katapult wird durch das Ziehen von Seilen bedient, ausgeführt durch Gefangene: dies scheint eine nicht sehr effektive Methode zu sein, es wurde jedoch den besten verfügbaren Quellen entnommen.

H Die Koreanischen Hilfstruppen, durch die unglückliche japanische Expedition in den mongolischen Dienst gezwungen, wurden der japanischen 'Mongolischen Invasionsschrift' entnommen; bemerke die aus dickem, handgenähtem Stoff hergestellten Mäntel und das grosse Schild aus Korbgeflecht und Bambus. Der Samurai wurde derselben Quelle entnommen und von erhaltenem Rüstzeug dieser Periode.

40